I DIDN'T SEE IT

The funniest Arsene Wenger quotes... ever!

by Gordon Law

About the author

Gordon Law is a freelance journalist and editor who has previously covered football for the *South London Press*, the *Premier League*, *Virgin Media* and a number of English national newspapers and magazines. He has also written several books on the beautiful game.

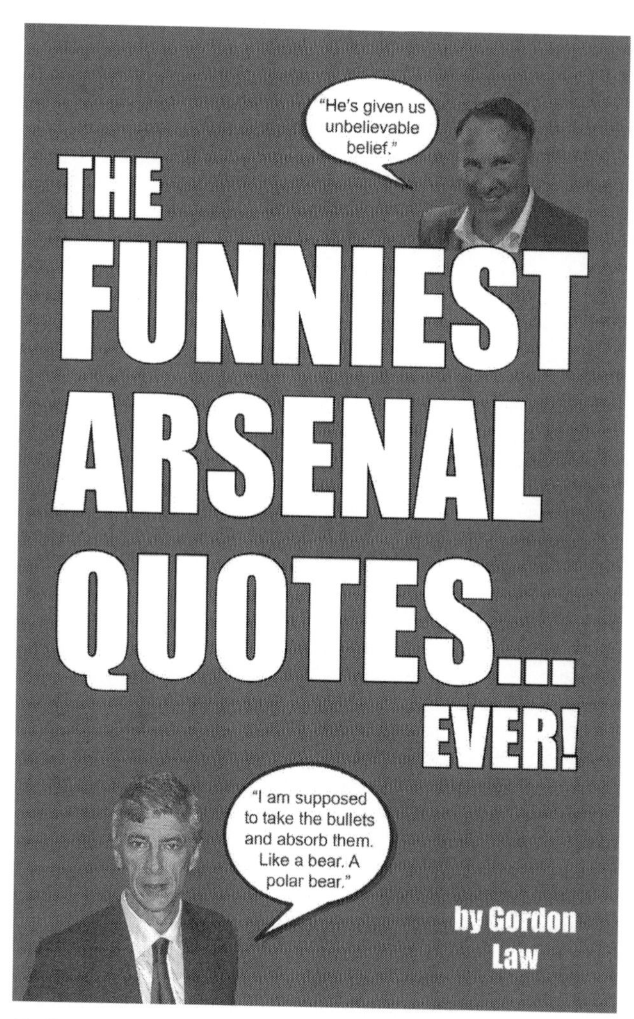
"He's given us unbelievable belief."
THE FUNNIEST ARSENAL QUOTES... EVER!
"I am supposed to take the bullets and absorb them. Like a bear. A polar bear."
by Gordon Law

gordonlawauthor@yahoo.com

Printed in the United States of America
ISBN-13: 978-1539813590
ISBN-10: 1539813592

Photo courtesy of: Mitch Gunn/Shutterstock.com.

Proofreaders: Stewart Coggin, Hywel Jones.

Contents

Introduction

There is no doubting Arsene Wenger's influence on English football and his achievements with Arsenal Football Club.

His innovative training and dietary methods, footballing philosophy, eye for young talent and the embracing of foreign stars yielded three Premier League titles and six FA Cups.

Arsenal's charismatic manager has also lit up press conferences with a plethora of hilarious, memorable and truly bonkers quotes since his arrival in England in 1996.

Wenger took on Sir Alex Ferguson in his mind games and the pair had an on-going feud for many years as they battled it out for football supremacy. The war of words between them was box office gold.

Things got more heated – and entertaining – when Jose Mourinho arrived on the scene and Wenger's rants at the so called 'Special One' made many headlines.

It's also the Frenchman's witty observations on football and life that have had us in stitches. Although his maths isn't great: "Of the nine red cards this season, we probably deserved half of them" and is prone to the odd innuendo: "Where his balls go, you will be quite surprised."

Probably the most famous Wenger sound bite is "I did not see it" after a misdemeanour by one of his players, which is also the title of this book. You'll find hundreds more hilarious quotes from Wenger and others in this unique collection. I hope you enjoy.

Gordon Law

I DIDN'T SEE IT

Wenger on referees

I DIDN'T SEE IT

"Frankly, I did not see what happened."

Arsene Wenger's now famous sound bite began after his second game in charge. Coventry keeper Steve Ogrizovic had to be taken off injured after a malicious tackle from Ian Wright, who was lucky not to be red carded

"The referee made a difference. All credit to him, he scored a good second goal for them. I was happy for him. He deserves a good mention."

He is not pleased with Borussia Dortmund's controversial penalty in a 2-1 defeat

"It is a great gesture by Fowler and I would like to give him an award of fair play. But if he got that I would also have to give the referee an award for stupidity."

Wenger on Liverpool's Robbie Fowler who asked referee Gerald Ashby to retract a penalty he had won against Arsenal at Highbury

"Sometimes, privately, I say, 'The referee was crap today,' but not publicly."

Wenger can also keep his counsel

I DIDN'T SEE IT

"I was surprised first of all that I was sent off for what I said. It's like if the speed limit is 60mph – sometimes you are not caught when you drive 70mph and sometimes you are caught when you drive 61mph. I drove 60.5mph."

Wenger is banished to the stands by the ref

"He wanted to protect himself as the referee was running his way."

The Frenchman explains why midfielder Emmanuel Petit manhandled ref Paul Durkin and was sent off

"I don't want to talk about the referee because I want to sit on the bench in the next game."

He is angry his side were handed five yellow cards against Barcelona

"It's a great profession being a referee. They are never wrong."

Wenger gets sarcastic

"The penalty decision was Old Traffordish."

Wenger is so angry at a typical Man United spot-kick that he makes up a word

"I watched it when I got home and it looked very bad. You ask 100 people, 99 will say it's very bad and the 100th will be Mark Hughes [Manchester City manager]."

Wenger is upset about Manchester City forward Emmanuel Adebayor's stamp on Robin van Persie

"Now we have a new problem – a goal that is cancelled for something that does not exist!"

He fumes at the Thierry Henry 'goal' against CSKA Moscow that was ruled out for 'hand ball'

Wenger on... referees

"Are the rules you can go first for the man when the ball is in the air and everybody decides it's not a foul, or do we make it a judo party and maybe everybody will be happy?"

The Gunners manager is not happy with a challenge

"I need to buy some Christmas presents and all these fines cost me, but the referee got some major decisions wrong."

Wenger is reluctant to criticise referees after a defeat to Manchester United

"It is difficult to lose the game on a wrong decision. It was offside and it is proven on TV. Why do we have to take it? I still don't think it's right. We have to do something about it. Yes, I am angry."

Wenger is left frustrated again

"[Giles] Grimandi made a head movement towards him but didn't touch him."

Le Professeur reckons his player did not headbutt his opponent

"Does he do it on purpose? Only God will be able to decide."

The manager reacts to Portsmouth's claims that Gunners star Robert Pires dived in order to win a penalty

"Sometimes I see it [a foul by an Arsenal player], but I say that I didn't see it to protect the players and because I could not find any rational explanation for what they did."

Wenger makes this shock confession that he lies to the media about seeing a controversial incident

I DIDN'T SEE IT

"We got the usual penalty for Manchester United when they are in a difficult position."

Wenger slams Mike Riley's decision to award United a spot-kick

Wenger on managing

"When you are a player, you think, 'Me! Me! Me!' When you are a manager, you think, 'You! You! You!'"

Wenger can make decisions from the bench but he knows it is up to the players

Reporter: "Why did you take Jack Wilshere off?"

Wenger: "It was 9.25, past his bedtime."

Wilshere was then aged just 16

"In my job, you expect to suffer. That's why when I go to hell one day, it will be less painful for me than you, because I'm used to suffering."

Wenger is used to the pain game

"If I had said in November that we will be in the semi-finals of the Champions League and FA Cup and go 21 games unbeaten, you'd have called an ambulance!"

Arsenal surprised many commentators by turning their 2008/09 season around

"If we have not got a game for a while, and we have lost, there are times when I have not gone out for days. It really hurts. People who live around you suffer with you, so the only thing I can do is try to get out of other people's way. I try to be like a dog who is sick – I go away into quarantine and come back when I'm cured!"

Wenger on coping with defeats

"Gerard [Houllier] is an open-minded and passionate man. I am the opposite: stubborn and stupid. But sometimes stupid behaviour makes you win."

Wenger's candid assessment on himself

"My secret is adapting to the country I am in. Here I eat roast beef and Yorkshire pudding. There are people who visit different countries and don't adapt. It is a must."

He adapted from his time living in Japan

"I am supposed to take the bullets and absorb them. Like a bear. A polar bear."

Wenger on criticism from the supporters

"The real revelation of a player's character is not in his social life but in how he plays. In my social life I can hide my real personality."

There is no hiding place on the pitch

"I don't kick dressing room doors, or the cat, or even journalists."

Wenger explains to the press how he copes with anger

"You live in a marginal world as a manager. I know three places in London: my house, Highbury and the training ground [in Hertfordshire].

On the discipline required to be a manager

"The face of the manager is a mirror to the health of the team."

Wenger uses this analogy to explain how he uses his personality to motivate players

"I can feel when I'm ready to lose it. Then I get my things and go home. I read a book for an hour or watch TV and come back a different man. It's what I call experience."

Wenger on how he is able to de-stress

"After a few years, managing in England is like working for the weather forecast office. You know when a storm is coming."

On managerial experience

"I never doubted, but when you don't win the game you wonder if you are right."

That sounds like a doubt

"When you work on the training ground every day, you don't notice where they're from. I don't even know where I'm from."

Wenger after his first XI – plus substitutes – contained no British players

"I like to read a book or talk to my wife or daughter, for an hour or so. But to have a whole day without thinking about football – that is impossible."

The manager is dedicated to the job

"The biggest things in life have been achieved by people who, at the start, we would have judged crazy. And yet if they had not had these crazy ideas the world would have been more stupid."

He refers to his revolutionary methods

"I am a thunderstorm protector."

Another weather analogy, this time on defending his players from the media

"It's not healthy to be negative. If today I am healthy, I know tomorrow I could die. But if I think like that there's more chance I will die."

The manager likes to think positive

"If you tell me that tomorrow I fight Mike Tyson, but you give an advantage to Tyson, I say, 'What's happening here?'."

Wenger on Man United profiting from their withdrawal from the FA Cup in 1999

"The fact that I say we will win it does not mean we have won it."

The manager on Arsenal's title aspirations

Reporter: "How long will Patrick Vieira stay?"

Wenger: "I am not a prophet."

"The biggest pressure is to have no pressure."

"It's like a child who is used to having ice cream whenever he wants. When it doesn't come when he asks, he tends to get confused and nervous."

On being knocked off the top of the table

"I started at 33 as a manager and sometimes I felt I wouldn't survive. Physically, I was sick."

It took a while for the manager to settle

"We have not come to a full stop. Maybe we have taken our foot off the accelerator slightly. That's all. It's not like a car that has hit a tree at 160mph."

The boss plays down losing a game

"I was cool, but internally very happy. If I had started to jump around the pitch, you would have had to send me to a hospital! I was close to doing it though – and when I start, I can't stop."

After the final game of Arsenal's unbeaten league season, a 2-1 win over Leicester

"A night without a game of football on television leaves me a little bit disillusioned. England is a good country because it gets dark early in winter, you go home and you're in an environment where you want to watch television. My wife understands my passion and is ready to pay the price."

Wenger the TV footie addict

"I changed a few habits [of the players], which isn't easy in a team where the average age is 30 years. At the first match the players were chanting, 'We want our Mars bars'. Then, at half-time I asked my physio Gary Lewin, 'Nobody is talking, what's wrong with them?' And he replied, 'They are hungry'. I hadn't given them their chocolate before the game. It was funny."

Wenger on his early days as Gunners boss, which included changing the players' diets

"I do not want to become a victim to the star system, where you go and buy a name but the player is dead."

On managers buying ageing stars

"Here he was not a gamble. He could come on as a substitute and there would be little expectation. There they will expect caviar – not sausages."

Wenger warns Nicolas Anelka about joining an Italian club

"I think in England you eat too much sugar and meat and not enough vegetables."

Diets were a concern for the manager

"I didn't know the English were good at swimming. I have been in this country for 12 years and I haven't seen a swimming pool."

Wenger didn't see it!

"What's really dreadful is the diet in Britain. The whole day you drink tea with milk and coffee with milk and cakes. If you had a fantasy world of what you shouldn't eat in sport, it's what you eat here."

Wenger on how English players ate in 1996

"I sometimes say to footballers' agents: 'The difference between you and me is that if there were no more money in football tomorrow, I'd still be here, but not you."

He's not a fan then...

"I am on earth to try to win games."

Wenger states his life mission

"I lived for two years in Japan and it was the best diet I ever had. The whole way of life there is linked to health. Their diet is basically boiled vegetables, fish and rice. No fat, no sugar. You notice when you live there that there are no fat people."

Wenger continues his diet obsession

"It was like Japan turning to France for a sumo manager."

He reflects on the appointment of a French manager in English football

"I've been infected by the English football virus. I'd miss that anywhere I went."

"I am in a job where you always look in front of you. Unfortunately, the older you get, the less distance there is in front of you."

The boss in pragmatic mood

"When you play your wife at tennis, you can love her to death but you still want to beat her."

Wenger doesn't like losing

"If you are living like an animal, what is the point of living? What makes daily life interesting is that we try to transform it to something that is close to art."

Wenger's aesthetically pleasing terms are a reflection of his philosophy

"Yes I like chips! But I try not to abuse it because I have a diet – I have to prepare like a player."

The boss reveals he does have a guilty pleasure

"Natural managers do not exist, I have never met one. If a natural manager exists, he must be in paradise."

Wenger's a natural

"I don't have a life outside football. When people ask me how I like London, I say, 'Where is London?'."

Wenger is dedicated to the job

I DIDN'T SEE IT

"One of the things I discovered in Japan was from watching sumo wrestling. At the end you can never tell who has won the fight, and who has lost, because they do not show their emotion because it could embarrass the loser. It is unbelievable. That is why I try to teach my team politeness. It is only here in England that everybody pokes their tongue out when they win."

Wenger on a management technique picked up from his time with Grampus Eight

Wenger on Fergie

"I was surprised to see Ferguson on the pitch because you can only play 11."

Wenger on the clash between Ian Wright and Peter Schmeichel which led to Alex Ferguson running on the pitch to protest

"He does what he wants. I will never answer questions about this man."

The manager sums up Ferguson

"I don't know if Alex Ferguson is rattled or will congratulate us if we do it, but the table doesn't lie. It's always right."

Speaking in May 2002, just before the Gunners win the league title

Wenger on... Fergie

“I don’t know about food throwing. I did not see if something was thrown – you’ll have to ask someone else because I don’t know. I don’t know what happened to Ferguson. Why don’t you ask Ferguson what happened to him. He can give you an answer. Why should I know what happened to Alex Ferguson’s shirt? Ferguson should know and he should say so.”

Wenger responds to suggestions that Ferguson appeared at the press conference in a change of suit after pizza was thrown on it in the tunnel area. Man United ended Arsenal’s 49-game unbeaten run at Old Trafford and the encounter was later dubbed ‘Pizzagate’ and ‘The Battle of the Buffet’

"[Alex] Ferguson's out of order. He has lost all sense of reality. He is going out looking for a confrontation, then asking the person he is confronting to apologise. He's pushed the cork in a bit far this time and lost a lot of credibility by saying what he said."

Arsene Wenger hits back at Ferguson who accused Wenger of confronting him with raised hands following United's 2-0 win, and failing to apologise for his players' bad behaviour in the tunnel, which led to pizza and soup thrown at Ferguson

"I have no gift for paranoia."

Wenger takes a swipe at Ferguson's mental state as the teams' rivalry intensifies

"What are all these asterisks in the newspaper?"

Wenger has a laugh about Ferguson's foul-mouthed rant at the press who suggested the £28m signing of Juan Sebastian Veron was a waste of money

"I would like to have signed Rio Ferdinand, but for £10m less."

The manager takes a pop at what he felt was an over-priced United signing

"What I don't understand is that he does what he wants and you are all at his feet."

To journalists regarding Ferguson

"When we meet sometimes – at airports or UEFA meetings, things like that – we don't hit each other."

Wenger plays down his rivalry with Ferguson

"Alex Ferguson's weakness is that he doesn't think he has any."

The manager in ironic mood

"If there is an apology, it must be coming by horseback."

Wenger after Ferguson claimed the Gunners "turned games into battles"

"Everyone thinks they have the prettiest wife at home."

Wenger responds in May 2002 to Ferguson who claimed Man United had been the best side in the league since Christmas that season

"We are confident, not stupid. I respect Alex but I am ignoring his comments in the same way I ignore all comments about Arsenal."

He dismisses Ferguson's suggestion that the Gunners' weakness was being over confident

"The managers will not be playing at 4pm today, although I'd like it if he [Ferguson] played. Maybe we could play one against one after the game."

Wenger loves to keep the rivalry going

"I think the word is respect. I can't say there is friendship on both sides."

Wenger replies to Ferguson's claim that the pair were on amicable terms

"That's a question you shouldn't ask me, but the referees."

Responding to reporters who asked about the prospect of facing United without Fergie

"I don't know whether he likes me or not. I don't know him well enough and these things don't worry me."

On his relationship with Ferguson

"Ferguson should calm down. Maybe it would have been better if he had put us against a wall and shot us."

Wenger replies to Ferguson's renewed claims that Arsenal are treated leniently

"What would I do if Alex wasn't around? I would have no one to keep me on my toes or to fight."

On Ferguson's decision to carry on

"I'm ready to take the blame for all the problems of English football if that is what he wants."

Wenger on Ferguson questioning Arsenal's lack of British players

"Any man who concentrates his energies totally on one passion is, by definition, someone who hurts the people close to him."

The boss on Ferguson's football obsession

"I'm not a great writer."

Wenger's retort to those who suggest he write to Ferguson to congratulate him on United's title win

Wenger on... Fergie

"He [Ferguson] doesn't interest me and doesn't matter to me at all. I will never answer to any provocation from him any more."

Has Ferguson got Wenger here?

"I prefer wine to whisky."

He refuses a post-match drink with Fergie

"Winning the title at Old Trafford will have no special significance."

Are you sure Arsene?

"I have no diplomatic relations with him."

Wenger admits the relationship is at a low

"He doesn't bother me. Perhaps the more sensitive can be affected. I understand his passion and if I get under his skin then that is good."

Wenger on his continuous battle of words with Ferguson

Fergie on Wenger

"He has no experience of English football. He's come from Japan. And now he's into English football and he is now telling everybody in England to organise their football. I think he should keep his mouth shut."

Ferguson is angry at Wenger for opposing the extension of the season with United facing their last four games in eight days

"They say he's an intelligent man, right? Speaks five languages! I've got a 15-year-old boy from the Ivory Coast who speaks five languages!"

He plays down Wenger's intelligence

Fergie on... Wenger

"In the tunnel Wenger was criticising my players, calling them cheats, so I told him to leave them alone and behave himself. He ran at me with his hands raised saying, 'What do you want to do about it?' To not apologise for the behaviour of the players to another manager is unthinkable. It's a disgrace, but I don't expect Wenger to ever apologise... he's that type of person."

The United manager reflects on 'Pizzagate'

"It's just the two of us. We'll probably ride out in the sunset together."

Ferguson reckons he and Wenger will end up becoming the best of friends

"He was livid. His fists were clenched. I was in control, I knew it. Anyway, the next thing I knew I had pizza all over me."

Ferguson on Wenger and 'Pizzagate' after his United team ended Arsenal's 49-game unbeaten run

"He never comes for a drink with the opposing manager after matches. He's the only manager in the Premiership not to do so. It is a tradition here. It would be good for him to accept the tradition."

The United boss thinks Wenger is rude not to engage in the customary post-match tipple

"Arsene Wenger disappoints me when he is reluctant to give credit to Manchester United for what we have achieved. And I don't think his carping has made a good impression on other managers in the Premiership."

Fergie is upset that Wenger refuses to give his players the credit they deserve for their success

"They are scrappers who rely on belligerence – we are the better team."

Ferguson slates Wenger's Arsenal as the Gunners claim the 2001/02 title after a 1-0 win at Old Trafford

"Arsenal's big advantage is that they can play Pat Rice at right-back and Arsene at centre forward on Saturday."

Ferguson on Arsenal resting players ahead of their 2009 Champions League semi-final against United

Wenger on the media

"If you ask me if I've lied to the press I must honestly say yes, but I had a clear conscience because it was for a good cause. I speak to the player beforehand and say, 'This is the story we're going to give'."

Wenger admits lying to the media to protect players, but says his conscience is clear

"If I go into a season and I say, 'For f*ck's sake, if we don't win anything, they will all leave,' I have already lost. The problem of the media is always to imagine the worst. The problem of the manager is always to imagine the best."

The usually mild-mannered Wenger swears at the press

"You [the media] have the right to say Arsenal are a dirty team and should have been fined £700,000. But you will never, ever find anyone in my club that I told to go out and kick someone in the game. If you find him, introduce him to me and I will face him."
Wenger after several of his players were punished by the FA following an encounter with Man United

"It's a Sky trial. There is one guy in a lorry who decided whether or not to show something again. It's not the FA."
Wenger slams the TV broadcaster claiming incidents involving Arsenal are more likely to be highlighted

The usually mild-mannered Wenger erupts at a pre-Bayern Munich media conference when a reporter mentions The Sun's story on Arsenal extending his contract. His epic rant at the reporters is hilarious...

Wenger: "That is the wrong information. I think I work for 16 years in England and I think I deserve a bit more credit than wrong information, that has only one intention, which is to harm. I look at you [Daily Mail reporter] not because you give the information. I do not know if it is you. I do not know where the information comes from."

Daily Mail: "Me?"

Wenger: "Yeah, why do you look at me?"

Daily Mail: "Because it's your press conference."

Wenger: "OK, thank you. I just thought you had given this information out."

Daily Mail: "No, I'm looking at you because it's your press conference."

Wenger: "OK, thank you very much."

Reporter: "The fans were very upset at going out of the cup [to Blackburn] at the weekend."

Wenger: "Look, here is a pre-match conference for the Champions League. If you want to talk about Saturday, that press conference has been made after the game. Can we get some questions about tomorrow's game? That would be very nice."

I DIDN'T SEE IT

Reporter: "The [Sun] story [about the renewal of his contract] was a positive one?"

Wenger: "Why does it just come out when we lose a big game? In your opinion? You think I am so naive that I don't see what is behind that? You think I am a complete idiot?"

Reporter: "What will happen beyond 2014?"

Wenger: "I am not completely sure that you are really interested. When we lost at home to Blackburn, I am not sure that is your first worry."

Reporter: "We would miss you!"

Wenger: "I am sure you would miss me when I am gone."

Reporter: "If this is your last chance to win a trophy this season..."

Wenger: [Sarcastically] "Thank you very much for that question. It's a long time that we didn't answer it."

Reporter: "But can you talk about your desire to bring back trophies to the club?"

Wenger: "Look, I have been accused of not taking seriously the FA Cup on Saturday... I have won four times the FA Cup. Who has won it more? Give me one name."

Reporter: "The question is about your desire to win the Champions League. It is there, isn't it?"

Wenger: "No, no. I want to lose it and I want to lose the game tomorrow, so you can all be happy."

And the heated exchanges end there. Ouch!

"Do not come always back with that same story. I think you lack a bit of creativity in the press at the moment and you follow a bandwagon. It's very boring. I don't go along with that (criticism). If you have an interesting question I will answer but apart from that let's not always come back to the same story."

Wenger snaps when asked if he will stick with David Ospina after his decision to play the keeper in the Champions League loss to Olympiakos was criticised

Interviewer: "How do you say 'screamer' in French?"

Wenger: "I'm sorry, I can't speak French anymore!"

"Stop that story or we stop the press conference."

Wenger was asked if Jose Mourinho was right in claiming he was the only Premier League manager not under pressure

"I've [managed] a thousand games, I work from morning to night every day in football, I do not need the opinion of somebody who has never worked in the game to know where we stand."

Wenger doesn't listen to what pundits say

I DIDN'T SEE IT

"I don't want to comment on that. I do my job and do my best for the club. Why should I create a rift? I have given you the answer. I leave it to you to judge. I try to be as good as I can be. You are all great managers! I read the newspapers every day and I can tell you that you are always great managers! You judge the game for the papers and I sit here and explain to you our game. How many games have you managed? I promise you if you manage one I will sit in the stands and chant: 'You know what you are doing!'"

Wenger blasts reporters when asked about the Gunners fans chanting: "You don't know what you're doing" against Aston Villa

"You can discuss every substitution. You think what you want. I do my job and I let people judge it. I do that every day and I do my best every day. I know why I do it."

Wenger continues his rant at the press after defeat at home to Villa

"You forget what you wrote last September, October, November. You have a little bit of Alzheimer's."

Wenger reminds the critical journalists that he led Arsenal to the Champions League after a bad run the previous season

I DIDN'T SEE IT

"This is English football like it really is, not like when you speak on TV and everyone wants to be nicey-nice. It's how football really is here in England and, the way you [the press] react, it is like you have never seen anything like it. Frankly, it's laughable."

Another backlash at the media's coverage of his team

Wenger on Mourinho

"If you would like to compare every manager you give each one the same amount of resources and say, 'You have that for five years'. After five years you see who has done the most."

Wenger barbs at Mourinho for having so much money to spend at Chelsea

"I know we live in a world where we have only winners and losers, but once a sport encourages teams who refuse to take the initiative, the sport is in danger."

The Frenchman has another dig at Mourinho's negative style of football

"He's out of order, disconnected with reality and disrespectful. When you give success to stupid people, it makes them more stupid sometimes."

Wenger threatens to take legal action against Mourinho for calling him a "voyeur"

"Take what Arsenal and Chelsea have won in the past eight years. I go with reality, with the football we play and the challenge we have ahead. I don't see especially that Chelsea play more English players than we do. Who have they produced, homegrown? Just one, John Terry."

He defends his decision to put out an all-foreign squad against Crystal Palace

"In hindsight I think I should not have reacted at all. It's not a way to behave on a football field. Did Mourinho provoke me? That is how I felt. I did not enter Chelsea's technical area."

Wenger is apologetic after pushing Mourinho on the touchline at Chelsea in 2014

"It is fear to fail."

After being asked why some managers [Mourinho] were playing down their title chances

"I think I just told you that the biggest thing for a manager is to respect other managers and some people have to improve on that. The rivalry is real. But it has to be respectful. I believe that the managers sometimes in the heat of the game, the passion gets out of control and when I'm guilty, I regret always."

Wenger wants Mourinho to show him a bit more respect

"It's impossible for us to match Chelsea's spending power – unless we find oil at Highbury."

On Roman Abramovich's riches which Mourinho has benefitted from

"Chelsea have already played twice against Man United, they could have sold him last week. I think if you want to respect the fairness for everybody, this should not happen."

Wenger is not happy Chelsea sold Juan Mata to Man United when the Blues had played their final match against them a week earlier and the Gunners had yet to face the Red Devils

"That's what people say when you don't win but, let's not forget you can be boring and lose as well. I believe big clubs have a responsibility to win but to win with style."

On talk that Chelsea play dull football

"When you see how it looks on television, I must say, what happened there is the best demonstration to think, 'Never do that again'. For yourself as well, never envisage to do that because it looks, frankly, horrible. It's a pity to see that from a big club."

Wenger – aiming an attack on Mourinho – suggested two of his Real Madrid players deliberately incurred second yellow cards at Ajax to avoid later suspensions in the Champions League knockout stages

I DIDN'T SEE IT

"You could say that our football was more attractive to watch but they are very efficient. They are a bit like a matador – they wait until the bull gets weak to kill him. They have the patience to wait as they have an experienced squad. When the bull has lost enough blood and becomes a bit dizzy, they kill it off."

Wenger on Chelsea's playing style under Mourinho

Mourinho on Wenger

"Wenger complaining is normal because he always does. Normally he should be happy that Chelsea sold a player like Juan Mata, but this is a little bit his nature. I think what is not fair is that his team always has the best days to play."

Mourinho on claims from Wenger that Chelsea selling Mata to Man United was unfair

"I'm not surprised, I'm not surprised. [Me] charged? Charged? If it was me it would have been a stadium ban."

The manager responds to journalists when it's suggested Wenger could be charged for shoving him

"Am I afraid of failure? He is a specialist in failure. I'm not. So if one supposes he's right and I'm afraid of failure, it's because I don't fail many times. So maybe he's right. I'm not used to failing. But the reality is he's a specialist because, eight years without a piece of silverware, that's failure. If I do that in Chelsea, eight years, I leave and don't come back."

Mourinho hits back at Wenger's view that the Chelsea boss has a fear of failure

"It's not easy. If it was easy, you [Arsenal] wouldn't lose 3-1 at home to Monaco [in the Champions League last 16]."

He replies to Wenger's suggestion that "it is easy to defend" in Europe

"At Stamford Bridge, we have a file of quotes from Mr Wenger about Chelsea football club in the last 12 months – it is not a file of five pages. It is a file of 120 pages."

The manager would be happy to see Wenger in court

"Instead of speaking about Real Madrid, Mr Wenger should speak about Arsenal and explain how he lost 2-0 against a team in the Champions League for the first time [Braga]. The history about the young kids is getting old now. Sagna, Clichy, Walcott, Fabregas, Song, Nasri, Van Persie, Arshavin are not kids. They are all top players."

Mourinho reacts to criticism from Wenger

"Wenger has a real problem with us and I think he is what you call in England a voyeur. He is someone who likes to watch other people. There are some guys who, when they are at home, have this big telescope to look into the homes of other people and see what is happening. Wenger must be one of them – it is a sickness. He speaks, speaks, speaks about Chelsea."

Mourinho makes his famous 'voyeur' accusation

"Many great managers have never won the Champions League – a big example is not far from us."

He has another pop at Wenger

"If you add up the amounts the clubs have spent in the last three or four years I think maybe you will find a surprise. Get a calculator. That is one of the easiest things to do. It leaves no space for speculation. If you want to be honest, objective and pragmatic it is the easiest job for a manager or a journalist to do. They have bought a fantastic goalkeeper and that is a position which is very important in a team. If you put Ozil plus Sanchez, plus Chambers, plus Debuchy you will maybe find a surprise."

Mourinho jabs Wenger for his levels of spending

"The English like statistics a lot. Do they know that Arsene Wenger has only 50 per cent of wins in the English league?"

Mourinho even uses stats to have a dig

"Unlike Arsenal, we sought success and tried to build it through a concept of the game using English players."

He attacks Arsenal's transfer policy

"I think boring is 10 years without a title – that's boring. If you support a club and you wait, wait, wait for so many years without a Premier League title, then that's boring."

Mourinho swipes at Wenger's title drought

"The last time I won a title was one year ago. It wasn't ten years ago, 15 years ago. One year ago. So if I have a lot to prove, imagine the others."

Mourinho pokes fun at Wenger in his first Man United press conference

"I could approach this job in a defensive point of view by saying 'the last three years the best we did was fourth and an FA Cup'."

The new United boss has another dig

Wenger on others

"Fulham gave us a kick in the you-know-whats and we responded."

The manager after a win over Fulham

"I don't think it's because of my eyes, my beautiful eyes!"

Wenger on why Thierry Henry stayed at Arsenal

"I'm just sorry West Ham lost a game because of my fault. Maybe I have to change my glasses."

Wenger hits back at Harry Redknapp who claimed Wenger got Paolo di Canio booked for diving

"You felt they had an angel behind their goalkeeper."

Wenger feels Blackburn Rovers keeper Brad Friedel benefitted from divine intervention in their victory

"There was no water underneath him but it was very nice."

The Gunners boss suggests Charlton's Matt Holland took a dive to win a penalty

"When Ian Wright is going well you must put him in jail to keep him out of the game."

Wenger on his talismanic striker

"Gerard Houllier's thoughts on the matter [international football] echo mine. He thinks that what the national coaches are doing is like taking the car from his garage without even asking permission. They will then use the car for ten days and abandon it in a field without any petrol left in the tank. We then have to recover it, but it is broken down. Then a month later they will come to take your car again, and for good measure you're expected to be nice about it."

Wenger agrees with the former Liverpool manager Gerard Houllier on losing players for international matches

"He looks like a nice boy but on the pitch it is not always fair behaviour."

Wenger on Ruud van Nistelrooy, who clashed with Patrick Vieira, which led to the Frenchman getting sent off

"He [Van Nistelrooy] always does it like he is innocent. Play football, my friend, and forget about all the rest."

Le Professeur is angry with the United star after a clash with Ashley Cole

"He's a basketball player."

The Gunners boss on Peter Crouch

"Peter Kenyon has no real influence on the Premiership title race because I don't consider him to be a football man. Trophies are not won in a directors' room but on the pitch."

Wenger on the Chelsea chief executive

"He's just training here but we're well equipped to handle it. We have everything that's needed, including mirror doors."

On David Beckham training with Arsenal

"I wish we could use 'Quincy' on his shirt, but they won't let us. I don't know how to pronounce his name – I've tried, but I can't."

Wenger on Quincy Owusu-Abeyie

“The Germans do well economically and we respect that. They are the only ones that make money in Europe. That’s why we’ve chosen a German.”

He explains why Per Mertesacker was given the job of collecting fines from the Arsenal players

“Do you really believe he didn’t see anything that was right in front of him? He says he didn’t see it but frankly, I don’t believe him, he is lying.”

Wenger to Tottenham boss Martin Jol for failing to spot Arsenal players on the ground in the build-up to their goal. Takes one to know one Arsene?

"He has that smell to be where he needs to be at the decisive moment. When there is chocolate to take in the box, he is there."

The manager on Julio Baptista

"If Chelsea want to buy Ashley Cole, you should be capable of finding the phone number of Arsenal Football Club."

Wenger on stories that Chelsea were having meetings with the Arsenal defender

"We know how Ruud van Nistelrooy behaves. He can only cheat people who don't know him well."

Wenger is clearly not a fan of the striker

"They seem to think they are above everything."

Wenger on Chelsea allegedly tapping up Ashley Cole in a hotel in plain sight in central London

"You ask me, 'Was he a fair player?' I say, 'No, I'm sorry, for me he was not a fair player.' I just think I respect him highly as a quality player. I did not like some things he did on the football pitch and I have the right to say that. It's not because you are older, suddenly, that you are a saint."

The Gunners boss on Paul Scholes

"They are a financially doped club. They have enhancement of performances through financial resources which are unlimited. For me, it's a kind of doping because it's not in any way linked to their resources."

Wenger on Chelsea's riches

"Everybody has a different opinion in this league and nobody is a prophet. I personally don't know who will win the league. I managed 1,600 games so, if Nani knows, he must be 1,600 times more intelligent than I am."

The Frenchman blasts Nani for dismissing Arsenal's title chances

"I think after every match he comes in with a bottle of champagne. He can open a shop now."

Yet another man-of-the-match performance by Dennis Bergkamp impresses Wenger

"I'm amazed how big Patrick Vieira's elbows are – they can reach players 10 yards away."

On the repeated accusations of foul play against his tough-tackling midfielder

"He has played for nearly every club in the world. It is absolutely amazing how much money he's moved for. He is, himself, a bank!"

On Nicolas Anelka after he joined Chelsea

"I should invite you sometimes to come into the dressing room and look at the legs of Alex Hleb after a game. You would be amazed."

Wenger is a fan of his player's legs

"Beckham is not a dirty player. Only in World Cups."

Le Professeur is in good spirits after an Arsenal win over United

"Martin Keown's movie career is probably over."

Wenger breaks the bad news after the defender required stitches following a clash against Wolves

"Spare me the articles about how nice Shawcross is because that was a horrendous tackle. People say we don't fancy the physical side of it, but this is the result. If you see a player getting injured like that, it's not acceptable."

He is angry at Ryan Shawcross after his tackle broke Aaron Ramsey's leg in 2010

"Jens changed his mind but wasn't quick enough to respond to his brain."

Wenger on a mistake by keeper Jens Lehmann that allowed Fulham's David Healy to score

"The Germans are the Germans."

Wenger dismisses the idea that Bayern Munich are not prepared for their Champions League match

"We won the trophy for the most unlucky team last year. Is it a trophy to finish 12th and win the Carling Cup? The real quality of a big club is to fight for the championship."

The manager takes a dig at Tottenham

"Ronaldo is the pepper in Real Madrid's sauce."

Wenger heaps praise on the Brazilian

"They are like snakes. They have spurts and in five minutes they can kill you."

He speaks about Champions League opponents Fiorentina

"Are United worthy? I don't know."

Wenger after losing the title to Man United

"I shook the hand of the manager and the assistant manager. How many people do I need to shake hands with? Is there a prescription?"

Wenger after Tottenham coach Clive Allen claimed the boss refused to shake his hand at the end of a north London derby

"If I wanted to sign a Madrid player my first call could be to the club, not the newspapers.
I expect a bit more class from Real Madrid."
Wenger after the Spaniards made their interest in Thierry Henry public

"I tried to watch the Tottenham match on television in my hotel yesterday, but I fell asleep."
The Arsenal boss fires a shot at Spurs

"He is like a PlayStation player. He is the best in the world by some distance."
Wenger on Lionel Messi

"How do you stop Rivaldo? You buy him the day before you play him."

The manager on trying to combat the Barcelona attacking star

"This guy is small but he has the mental strength of a mountain."

Wenger on Eduardo

"If Ken Bates is thinking of suing me then he must be a very sensitive boy."

Wenger on Chelsea chairman Ken Bates who issued a threat to him after the Frenchman claimed the Blues were stoking up players' wages

"He always begins the game like he hasn't played football for three days."

Wenger on Cristiano Ronaldo

"[Manuel] Almunia took the criticism and responded with one word – his performance on the pitch."

The Arsenal boss uses five words instead of one

"He's focused and determined, but also very young. I don't think he even shaves yet."

Wenger on Jack Wilshere, aged 16

"He was sacked for his beliefs. Still, 500 years ago you could be burnt at the stake for that. At least now you are only sacked. Things have improved a little bit."

Speaking about the firing of Glenn Hoddle as England manager for his views on reincarnation

"Don't mind and don't care."

Wenger after being asked by reporters about Tottenham Hotspur's European exit to Basel

"They are like the lion. He has to catch the animal in the first 200 metres. If he doesn't get there, after he's dead. They are these kind of killers. When they go, it is to kill and after they have to stop."

Wenger compares Alexis Sanchez and Jamie Vardy to the jungle cat

Wenger on discipline

"They have my credit card number and we will say, 'How much do you need this week? Let's do it.'"

Wenger loves his trips to face the FA's disciplinary panel

"I don't know how Mr Bean can stop me from saying what I believe is right unless he puts me in jail."

FA compliance officer Graham Bean – an ex-policeman – called Wenger to discuss his comments after he accused Charlton midfielder Neil Redfearn of cheating

Wenger on... discipline

"If you look at our red cards, it's mostly a case of provocation. You can say that winding someone up is clever but you'll never convince me it's fair. Unfortunately it has worked for 52 players."

Wenger explains how he has over half a century of dismissals as Gunners manager

"Why don't they put us in Division One?"

Wenger on Arsenal's disciplinary record ahead of meeting an FA panel

"I know you will laugh when I say I didn't see it."

Wenger brings out his famous line after Oleg Luzhny gets sent off

"The background looks like a lot of red cards."

Wenger at the unveiling of Arsenal's new-look club crest

"When we go to the FA disciplinary hearings, we are used to coming back with a heavy bag."

He accepts the club are often fined heavily

"We should not have reacted like we did. But I find the sensitivity of this country very selective. Suddenly the whole of England is so shocked, as if there's never any violence in your society."

On Arsenal being charged by the FA after the 'Battle of Old Trafford' in 2003

"If you believed in a conspiracy, you would become paranoid and the next step after that is schizophrenia, a feeling that the world is against you."

Wenger reflects on his side's discipline issues

"Some clubs can never be caught. It's like you say it's only for the Mercedes that the speed limit counts. Everyone else can drive as they want."

The boss thinks Arsenal are unfairly treated at the 'Battle of Old Trafford'

"Even if you hang us, it is not enough for some people. They want us hung twice, and in Hyde Park, in front of the whole country."

Wenger responds to Alex Ferguson who claimed Arsenal's punishments were not strong enough

"Perhaps Dennis had a nervous reaction."

After Dennis Bergkamp appeared to stamp on Blackburn's Nils-Eric Johansson

"Of the nine red cards this season we probably deserved half of them."

Wenger's sums don't add up

"He's not always the devil people think he is. He's gone 19 games now without a booking – it's a long time, too long, he's too soft!"

The Arsenal manager on Patrick Vieira

"When I heard the sanctions, I couldn't believe it. I feel like I have killed someone. I didn't even insult anybody. I just behaved as I think I had to."

Wenger was handed a £100,000 fine and 12-match touchline ban for 'holding' an official after the Sunderland game

I DIDN'T SEE IT

"It was weird, spectacular. I didn't even know where to go... just because I kicked a bottle of water, I didn't say a word to anybody. And it was quite a good kick."

Wenger after being sent to the stands at Old Trafford

"It's not my job to judge what people do. I am not a policeman."

When asked what he thought about Thierry Henry confronting referee Graham Poll against Newcastle United

Wenger on... discipline

"Durkin is Durkin. What can we do about him."

On referee Paul Durkin who sent off Sol Campbell at Southampton

"As long as I'm not behind bars."

Wenger replies to reporters who asked if he'd be taking his weekly press conference after leaving his appeal hearing at the FA

"I saw Martin Keown defending himself with his elbow."

On the clash between his defender and Leeds United striker Mark Viduka

"When you say in French that you have no personality, it's not a compliment, but it's also not an insult."

Wenger on Patrick Vieira's charge for calling referee Andy D'Urso "a nobody with no personality"

Others on Wenger

"I think Arsene Wenger should have been fined several times over for his team's behaviour – 40 sendings-off in his first five years as manager is nothing short of a disgrace."
The great Brian Clough was not a fan of the indiscipline he felt Wenger's side showed in the early years

"I'm not wearing Mr Wenger glasses. I really didn't get a good view of the incident."
West Brom manager Tony Mowbray

"We sometimes think of Arsene Wenger as a general media population."
Rodney Marsh

"Arsene Wenger built a stadium at Arsenal, though he didn't actually build a stadium."

Tony Gale

"He arrived unnoticed at the training ground. A meeting was called, the players filed in and in front of us stood this tall, slightly built man who gave no impression whatsoever of being a football manager."

Lee Dixon on his first impression of Wenger

"When Arsene first came to Arsenal, we called him Clouseau and then Windows because of those boffin's glasses."

Tony Adams

"The biggest b*llocking I got in six years of playing for Arsene was when we lost a game and he came in and said, 'I cannot stand for this. This is not acceptable'."
Tony Adams

"On a great day in American electoral history, I would like to remind him of Abraham Lincoln's great quotation: 'You can fool some of the people all of the time and all of the people some of the time. But you cannot fool all of the people all of the time'."
Stoke boss Tony Pulis talks about Wenger on the day Barack Obama was elected as the new US President

Others on... Wenger

"He really is something. I love him. He is Sir Arsene Wenger. But he likes having the ball, playing football, passes. It's like an orchestra, but it is a silent song. I like heavy metal more."

Borussia Dortmund manager Jurgen Klopp

"At the moment I'm just swallowing it all as part of the humiliation but I think – and this is aimed at my dear manager – one shouldn't humiliate players for too long."

Jens Lehmann on being dropped by Wenger

"I'll give you an Arsene Wenger answer – I didn't see the sending off."

Acting Preston manager Kelham O'Hanlon

"I don't think we need foreign managers running national sides. I've got nothing against foreign managers, they are very nice people. Apart from Arsene Wenger."

Tony Pulis

"I played with him for six years. I've met him a few times. The more I got to know him the less I know him. I haven't a clue how that man thinks, how he works. He's difficult to fathom."

Tony Adams

"Arsene Wenger and I enjoy pitting our witses against each other."

Blackburn manager Sam Allardyce

"I can't comment on the sending off [of Dion Dublin] without sounding like Mr Wenger. It was a hot day and the sun was in my eyes."

Leicester manager Micky Adams

"The English manager I most admire is Arsene Wenger. Even if he is not English."

Luiz Felipe Scolari

"The new manager [Arsene Wenger] has put me on grilled fish, grilled broccoli, grilled everything. Yuk!"

Ian Wright

I DIDN'T SEE IT

"Mr Wenger's a very clever man but I have to say what he said is crap."

Sunderland manager Peter Reid after Wenger claimed one of his players tried to get Patrick Vieira sent off

"Wenger has an English mind but also a German mind, which is very disciplined."

Glenn Hoddle

"He says he didn't see me or hear me but he's two bob he is, two bob."

Tottenham coach Clive Allen claimed Wenger refused to shake his hand after the north London derby

"Arsene Wenger has put me down a few times. The annoying thing is, he does it intelligently and I hate that. Sometimes I want to punch him on the nose."

Tony Adams

"We know that Arsene Wenger likes the look of [Andrei] Arshavin, but I like the look of Angelina Jolie. It doesn't mean you get what you want."

Dennis Lachter, the agent of the Zenit St Petersburg midfielder

"He's given us unbelievable belief."

Paul Merson on Arsene Wenger

"I think Arsene's a great manager. The trouble is that if you ever make a valid point about him and the club, it's like criticising the Pope. Everybody gets up in arms."

Frank McLintock

"I've got to play for a Frenchman? You have to be joking."

Tony Adams recalls his reaction to Wenger's appointment

"If Wenger is still here in 10 years and Arsenal haven't won any trophies, will he still be here?"

Steve Claridge

"There was one time he wouldn't shake hands with me at Highbury because we got a draw. I saw him ripping his tie off and throwing it on the floor in anger. He takes it all very personally and has an air of arrogance. He's not one for inviting you into his office for a drink after the game. The more I wound him up, the more I liked it."

Sam Allardyce on his rivalry with Wenger

"The fact he personally contacted me and made so much effort to recruit me, it has seduced me."

Bacary Sagna is in love

I DIDN'T SEE IT

"One of the first things Arsene Wenger did at Arsenal was to make sure players couldn't get pay-per-view in hotels. If players are exciting themselves quite a few times then it's going to affect their physical condition."

Tony Adams

"Arsene Wenger uses the FA Cup to bleed his youngsters."

Alvin Martin thinks Wenger is harsh on his players

Wenger on the game

"I'm very excited with this team because they are 'playerish' – if there is such a word they love to play."

Wenger makes up yet another new word

"When I arrive at the gates of heaven, the Good Lord will ask, 'What did you do in your life?' I will respond, 'I tried to win football matches'. He will say, 'Are you certain that's all?' But, well, that's the story of my life."

The manager's philosophy

"We didn't think he would play on Sunday because he was suspended – that makes me think he has all the qualities to join Arsenal!"

Wenger on new signing Jose Antonio Reyes

"When I was younger I was much more excited on the bench. But now I have some problems to get up quickly."

Ooh, er...!

"He will have to speak to Jesus. We cannot afford those wages."

Wenger on Patrick Kluivert's salary demands – and he later joins Newcastle

"I have no regrets, but it is a big surprise to me because he cancelled his contract to go abroad. Have you sold Portsmouth to a foreign country? No."

He is surprised to hear of Sol Campbell's decision to join Portsmouth

"I gave [Cristiano] Ronaldo a shirt with his name on the back. I'm disappointed that I seduced only his mum."

Wenger on trying to sign Ronaldo as a teenager

"England boss Sven-Goran Eriksson was here, so who did he watch then? Has he signed for a different country?"

Wenger is baffled as to why Eriksson was watching a Gunners side with no English players against Crystal Palace

"It's like you wanting to marry Miss World and she doesn't want you. I can try to help you but if she does not want to marry you what can I do?"

Wenger after Jose Antonio Reyes said he wanted to leave the Gunners

"I am not against being pragmatic, because it is pragmatic to make a good pass, not a bad one. If I have the ball, what do I do with it? Could anybody argue that a bad solution like just kicking it away is pragmatic just because, sometimes, it works by accident?"

On his footballing style

"Ideally, you do not want to play an English team because it is not really Europe."

Wenger on who he wants to avoid in the Champions League draw

"Despite the global warming, England is still not warm enough for him."

Wenger bids farewell to Spanish midfielder Jose Antonio Reyes

"If they do what they like to do, then we will expose ourselves."

Erm... please don't

"We even watched [Cesc] Fabregas in training at Barcelona. How did I do that? With a hat and a moustache."

Covert scouting from Wenger

"If people come to your window and talk to your wife every night, you can't accept it without asking what's happening."

Wenger when asked about Chelsea's interest in Ashley Cole

"The fire is always ready. But now it looks as though you're burned on the village green quicker than ever."

On the frequency of managers getting sacked

"Where his balls go, you will be quite surprised."

The manager on Denilson's attributes

"A football team is like a beautiful woman. When you do not tell her so, she forgets she is beautiful."

Wenger on praising players

"If you ask if I'd rather see Chelsea or Man United win the title, then I will answer Arsenal."

On claims from Jose Mourinho that he'd rather see United win the title than Chelsea

"You've certainly tried to go out with a girl, but find she has chosen someone else. You don't commit suicide."

After Wenger's bid for Luis Suarez was rejected by Liverpool

"You have to be a masochist to be an international manager."

Wenger rules out becoming boss of a national side

"If I give you a good wine, you will see how it tastes and after you ask where it comes from."

Wenger defends his foreign transfer policy

"[Married players] have more emotional stability unless they are married to a nightmare."

Wenger on marriage

"Why do you go for a foreign guy? It is like you go to war and say, 'Now we choose a general from Portugal or a general from Italy'. Would that cross your mind? Never."

Wenger is perplexed by Fabio Capello's appointment as England manager

"If you buy a man who is half-dead, everybody may be happy off the field, but on the field you'll have major problems."

OK, then...

"We have Kieran Gibbs as a doubt too. He has a little groin problem."

Ooh, er missus!

"I do not think about the national team too much because footballistically it is not of too much interest."

More word creation from Wenger

"I said it was a no-brainer. I'm just sorry he didn't cost £25m."

On signing Mathieu Flamini on a free and refusing to bow to the demands of the fans and media to spend big

"We were considering Ruud van Nistelrooy and Francis Jeffers and, in the end, we went for Jeffers."

Wenger might have made a bad call here

“Maybe people will be surprised that I have signed an Englishman but I looked at his quality and not his passport. Francis is a ‘fox in the box’.”

The manager on striker Francis Jeffers

“It was very difficult to get in touch with the French national team after the World Cup. You know the French!”

Wenger on the trouble he faced trying to speak with France about ‘over-using’ Thierry Henry

“Davor has a left leg and a nose in the box.”

The manager on Davor Suker

I DIDN'T SEE IT

"I knew my players were ready. After a few years, you just know. It's like working for the weather forecast: you have a feeling whether it will rain or not."

Wenger after Arsenal beat Chelsea

"In international competition, sometimes not conceding a goal is one step better than scoring one."

Nice logic there, Arsene

"I don't know who will win the title now – and I don't care."

Wenger sulks after Arsenal concede three late goals to lose at Wigan

"I must consider whether what looks very high in August is very high in November."

Wenger on transfer fees

"Sometimes if a player is really dirty on the field but outside in life he is so nice, at important times in his life he will become like he is on the field."

Wenger says a player's real personality comes out on the pitch

"I am not happy or unhappy with him."

Wenger tries to clear up reports a rift between him and Thierry Henry

"It will take a maximum of two meetings to decide things. I say that because it always takes time. It's like a girl being told never to say 'yes' on a first date."

Wenger on extending his contract

"When you're dealing with someone who has only a pair of underpants on and you take them off, he has nothing left. He is naked. You're better off trying to find him a pair of trousers to complement him rather than change him."

He doesn't want to stifle creativity and take away a player's flair

“If you have a child who is a good musician, what is your first reaction? It is to put them into a good music school, not in an average one. So why should that not happen in football?”

UEFA president Michel Platini and FIFA president Sepp Blatter suggested top clubs’ pursuit of young players was akin to “child slavery” and “child trafficking”

“No matter how much money you earn, you can only eat three meals a day and sleep in one bed.”

Wenger reacts to Nicolas Anelka’s lucrative transfer to Real Madrid

"It's a question of what you like most: vanilla or chocolate ice cream. Both are good. I just like vanilla more."

On the Premier League (vanilla) vs the Champions League (chocolate)

"Ian [Wright] has a slight hamstring but [David] Platt has a big hamstring."

Revealing team news from Wenger

"Since I've been in football there has been a basic question to face. Are you pretty or are you efficient? It's as if you have to choose."

Wenger believes that style and substance can go together

"With a team you live in a tunnel and sometimes you have to go down and flirt with hell to see how much you can deal with that, so that you become stronger. But you go quickly to hell and very slowly to heaven."

Wenger after Arsenal's win over Bolton

"When people say, 'Arsenal didn't fancy it', what didn't they fancy? Getting tackled from behind?"

Wenger referring to Stoke City

"As long as no-one scored, it was always going to be close."

Interesting observation from Wenger

"If you eat caviar every day it's difficult to return to sausages."

Wenger on boos by the Arsenal fans after a 1-1 draw with Middlesbrough in 1998 – just six months after the Gunners had won the double

"For me, a doctor is first and foremost a doctor. He does not wear a club shirt... A doctor does not go to an accident and asks a victim if he is a Manchester United or Arsenal fan before he treats him."

Wenger gets annoyed after members of Arsenal's medical staff were dismissed by England

"The fifth goal definitely killed the game."

Wenger states the obvious with the Gunners 5-0 up after 52 minutes

"We could be playing snowball instead of football in Moscow."

Wenger on playing Russian outfit Spartak

"It's obviously not our dream to have to go to Blackburn. It's hardly the most fantastic place touristically."

Wenger is not happy about Arsenal heading to the Lancashire town for an FA Cup replay

I DIDN'T SEE IT

"By the time you read this we'll have had a scan on Fabregas. His foot blew up after the game and that's not the best sign."

Wenger on Fabregas' dangerous foot

"Sometimes you have to swallow the unswallowable."

Right, then!

33445609R00083

Printed in Poland
by Amazon Fulfillment
Poland Sp. z o.o., Wrocław